Raw & Unfinished

d. r. sanchez

Copyright © 2018 Debra R. Sanchez

All rights reserved. This book or any portion thereof may not be reproduced, performed or used in any manner whatsoever without the express written permission of the publisher or author except for the use of brief quotations in a book review.

Printed in the United States of America

First Printing 2018

ISBN 13: 978-1-948894-00-5
ISBN10: 1-948894-00-9

Tree Shadow Press
www.treeshadowpress.com

For reproduction permission, contact:
Debra R. Sanchez
dbrsanchez@gmail.com

Cover art by Debra R. Sanchez.
Author photo by Melissa Schneider.

DEDICATION

*To my family and my writing network,
thank you for your support and encouragement.
You let me be me.*

CONTENTS

Acknowledgments

I

Tomorrow's Yesterdays	1
Controlled	2
Generations Unseparated by Time and Distance	4
Getting Ready	5
It Was Inevitable	6
The One	8
Mother's Language	9
Identity Denied	10
Unshelved	12
Quotes from My Mom for Future Reference	13

II

Baptisms and Burials	17
Cat Again – Never Again	18
Of Death and Flies and Summer	20
Getting the Picture	21
Google Earth	22
Hope	24
Glory to the Outraged People	26

The Still Nest	27
Seasonal Threads	28
Slip	29
We Can Never Go Back	30
Coverage	31
Layers	32

III

3rd Eye	35
The Perfect Words	36
Reflections of a Chaotic Life – Uncut & Submitted	38
Burn	42
Thoughts While Driving	43
Unsettled	44
Powerless	45
Dark Vision	46
Protected Prison	47
There Isn't As Much	48
NOTES	49

ACKNOWLEDGMENTS

A special thanks to those who
inspired the words,
improved the words,
encouraged the words,
approved the words.

This book would not be possible without the support of the special people in my writing network, especially Laura Lovic-Lindsay and Kerry E.B. Black. Thank you for helping chose what to include, and more importantly what not to include. Thank you to Ruth Ochs Webster for nudging me to pick this final title.

A very special thanks goes to my writing mentor and friend, Jim Perkins, who may remember some of these from the time I spent in his poetry workshop.

I also want to express my thanks to my mother, who inspired some of the included poems. After I read them aloud to her, she gave her permission to publish them. You truly are an inspirational woman, Mom.

Most of the poems included in this book have either been previously published or won awards over the years. A list of details can be found in the NOTES section in the back of the book.

PART

I

TOMORROW'S YESTERDAYS

Reflections of

Who we come from
Who we are
Who we will be

Comprehension of the past
Contemplation of the present
Consideration of the future

Those before me, some gone, some remain
Those with me, some near, some distant
Those after me, some here, some yet to be born

Who will look back
From the mirror of the future?
Perhaps, some long forgotten face from the past.

CONTROLED

She grew up not far from the cemetery,
near the turn of the century,
above the bath house,
that was controlled by her parents.

Jane loved Bob.
Bob loved Jane.
They longed to be married.

She was raised to obey,
and to teach Sunday School,
and maybe, someday, in an all-girls' school.
She was controlled by her parents.

Jane was Irish.
Bob was German.
They were forbidden to be married.

She was the dutiful daughter,
until her parents went to the cemetery,
during the Depression years.
She was no longer controlled by her parents.

Jane was free.
Bob was not.
He had found someone else to marry.

She worked as the secretary of her church,
and taught Sunday School, and at an
all-girls' church summer camp.
She was controlled by her destiny.

Jane met Tom.
Tom loved Jane.
They decided to be married.

She was older than her groom.
Medical issues put her past conception,
so they adopted one of her brother's children.
They were controlled by circumstances.

Jane loved Bob.
Tom was Irish.
They knew that they would stay married.

They raised their family on Rosetta street.
They took in two foster sisters, and his aging mother,
creating a nearly all-girl home.
They were controlled by life.

Jane stood by Tom.
Tom supported Jane.
For nearly 40 years they were married.

The girls grew up and married,
with children of their own,
between them a boy and three girls,
controlled by nothing but the future.

Jane buried Tom.
Tom freed Jane.
She was glad to no longer be married.

Over the next dozen years she connected, by mail,
with her past, and told the oldest granddaughter
to be sure to marry for love, and
not be controlled by anything.

Jane loved Bob.
Bob remembered Jane.
They were never meant to be married.

GENERATIONS UNSEPARATED BY TIME AND DISTANCE

She was with me when she died,
With thousands of miles
And the Caribbean Sea between us.

Maybe it was because I was her favorite,
And the power of her love
Evaporated the distance.

Or maybe her power came from
Being the oldest offspring of
The seventh son of a seventh son

Who was born February 29, 1864, in Ireland.
People sought his power, true power,
To heal, to calm, to grow, to see, to know.

Thirteen years after her death
She visited the next generation
With her blue eyes and pink hair.

Or so claimed my 3 year old at the time,
As she spoke through raging fever,
To the air above her.

Decades have come and gone
And her words from the last 3 a.m. visit
Still resonate in my head.

"I am fine now. I was just so weary."
When the call came hours later,
I was not surprised. I already knew.

GETTING READY

The restless child had to be tied to a tree
To keep her from getting lost to the creek
Getting ready to be a handful

Endless days of childhood pranks
Shearing the cousins, dumping the wash tub,
Getting ready for years of fun

Sneaking out windows
To ride off with friends
Getting ready for nights to come

To avoid conflict about paying for a wedding
She eloped with the man she loved
Getting ready for marriage

They met secretly for months, still living at home,
Hoping nature would not catch them
Getting ready for life

After 60 years, 3 children, and 6 grandchildren,
They began taking trips,
Fixing up the house, new roof, new carpet (twice)
Getting ready for old age

Disease took him in his late 80's
But at 90, she was still defiant, still
Getting ready for old age

A broken foot was just enough to
Slow her down at 94
At 97 she was ready

6 months shy of a century, she met The End

IT WAS INEVITABLE

She was a criminal, not for
      the motorcycle she stole,
but rather, for the red dress she wore.

He did not arrest her
      as his duty demanded,
but rather, he let her change.

She, the lively rebel,
      carefree, joyful
and full of vitality.

He, the stern authority,
      disciplinarian, serious
and full of propriety.

It was inevitable.

He built their home
      of carved lava rock
with his own hands.

She bore their eight children
      all in the same room
with little more than love.

He had to leave in 1959
      forced by economics
to find a better future.

She remained behind until 1963
      sending the older ones, in time,
to join their father in work.

It was inevitable.

She stayed at home,
    as custom dictated,
to raise their six surviving children.

He worked long hours,
    six days a week,
to support them all.

She grew older, more graceful,
    never a grey hair,
with help from a bottle.

He grew more dignified, stoic,
    hair a silver white,
with no signs of thinning.

It was inevitable.

He finally retired,
    ready to go back
and live in the house he built.

She packed only what she
    thought they might need
and left the rest behind.

He was seldom sick,
    throughout his life,
but he was the first to go.

She had struggled with health,
    clinging to life,
but lingered only two months more.

It was inevitable.

THE ONE

She knew before she met me
That she'd love me unto death.
How could she not?
I was the one,
Chosen by her son.
I was born 23 minutes
After her birthday.
She taught me to make *arepas*.

I knew before I met her
That I'd love her unto death.
How could I not?
She was the one,
Chosen by my son.
I was born 23 minutes
After her birthday.
I taught her to make *arepas*.

Three generations of men
The father, the son, the grandson,
All of distinct character,
Married women who, though
Separated by decades,
Were born within 24 hours of each other.

It was inevitable.

MOTHERS LANGUAGE

My mother gave me language,
taught me to say the words,
the good and the bad,
happy and sad,
showing me
how to
go.

Then,
one day
I went far
away and had
to find other words
in the land of my spouse.
His mother gave me language.

IDENTITY DENIED

The only name she knows to be real
has just three letters.
That is who she is,
who she has always been.

Forced to change families at four,
not understanding why
siblings turned into cousins,
and Mother and Aunt reversed.

Unsure of who she was,
and longing to belong,
she married too quickly,
to try to find herself.

It lasted a while,
but wasn't meant to be.
Her children nearly grown,
she was forced into life alone.

She thought she found
the one she was meant for.
So she married again,
with another new name.

When the marriage ended in death,
she learned, at the grave,
that the name she now used
was not her late mate's.

A victim of lies,
for nearly a decade,
she felt shattered,
unable to trust.

The only identities she knows to be real
are mother, and grandmother,
and the three-letter first name
that she uses at meetings.

UNSHELVED

she always lived...
...a sheltered life
...a shelled life
...a shelved life

and then she...
...left that life
...felt new life
...lives her life

QUOTES FROM MY MOM FOR FUTURE REFERENCE

She said

I didn't realize who I was
I didn't know that I was that
important and
what all I accomplished
I wonder if maybe that
was someone else
I remember doing those things
so I guess
maybe I was more
important than I realized
And now I just sit and do nothing

I reflect

Looking at her life and her words
Looking at my own life
They are also my words

PART

II

BAPTISMS & BURIALS

Families
Ties that bind
Beginnings and
Beyond
Life is the
Dash

Make dash-ing memories while you can

Birth
Baptism
Marriage
Death
Burial
Happen to most

Birth and Death
To all

CAT AGAIN – NEVER AGAIN

1
A cat has nine lives.
Some cultures say seven.
I had a kitten with three lives.
Three deaths.

She escaped one night.
After the guard dogs were released.
It was long ago.
Far away.

I can still see her.
Golden tiger-striped body.
Torn open.
One leg gone.

We buried her out back.
She returned the next morning.
Missing another leg.
Ear gone.

The stench of death.
Unbearable in tropical heat.
I put her in a bag, in a box.
Buried her again.

In the morning, she was there.
Flies and maggots feeding.
On rotting flesh.
Tufts of fur.

Choking back tears.
And vomit.
I gathered the pieces.
Again.

In a bag, in an air-tight can.
In a box.
In a bag.
Buried deep.

For weeks I dreaded opening the door.
Terrified she'd be back.
But after the third day.
She arose no more.

> 2
> Another kitten
> Another dog
> Still long ago
> Still far away
>
> Unrelenting nightmares,
> replicating the reality
> of the massacre.
> The kitten turned inside out.
> Gruesome sight magnified
> by reading *Pet Sematary*,
> when your child is the age
> of the child in the book.
>
> This time
> I was spared
> the agony
> of another
> resurrecting cat.

OF DEATH AND FLIES AND SUMMER

The buzzing is back
Fruit flies invade the kitchen
Honey on a little plate
Wine vinegar in a small cup
My desire to kill is strong

Damned little flies make my head spin
Make me gag

Like the summer of flies
The summer the fire-red sunset
Laced its way through the curtain
of flies on my bedroom window

The summer I cried myself to sleep most nights
The summer before senior year of high school
The summer my Irish Setter exploded internally after
a botched procedure
The summer of divorce
The summer of death

Of my dog
Of the two hundred and seventy-seven flies I smashed on my window
Of my parent's marriage
      Of childhood

GETTING THE PICTURE

After life in rural high school,
before college in the mountains of country roads,
my summer was spent on a corner in Queens.

My daily commute a subway, a bus, a transfer,
and ten block walk to a lot near a hospital bus stop,
where I watched employees and patients.

Some were safe, others harassed, few threatened,
yet I was unafraid, protected by the window locks,
of the FotoHut with conditioned air, and no phone.

Just enough room to stand, four feet wide, six deep,
drop off bins under the counter in front of me, film and flash,
inventory above, stacked to the ceiling, within easy reach.

I locked up for grilled cheese with pickle and bacon,
for daily lunch at the diner across the street, and an egg cream,
which has no egg, has no cream.

Business was slow, the delivery driver stopped,
mid afternoon to pick up, to drop off,
what the customers dropped off, picked up.

Books and solitaire to fill the between,
and I honed my ability to pry open seals on envelopes,
careful that none witnessed me examining the contents.

It was 1978, no selfies, no smart phones or computers,
people used cartridges and rolls to capture their exposures,
and trusted their private secrets to curious teens.

GOOGLE EARTH

1

Images of my childhood home
Clear, crisp, sharp
Like my memories of that time

The maple in the front yard is gone
No more climbing
To beat out the rhythms of life
'Til we scarred the bark
No more tire, swinging
For us to spin ourselves silly
And drunkenly collide into the trunk

There is a new garage; we never had one
And a new house in the vacant lot
Where I used to blaze trails and build forts
Among the tall grass and apple trees
Half of the pines are still there
That sap-stained our hands and clothes
Where I made campfires in empty coffee cans
Where I climbed to the top
Where my brother got stuck

Coopers' house across the street is gone
The other Coopers' house next door is still there
So is the tree we tied David to
We knew it was wrong
But we were young enough to not understand why
The pipeline up Raccoon Hill is still clearly visible
Where Ritchie rode his bike into the trees

2
Houses of my early motherhood
Clear, crisp, sharp
Like my memories of that time

The tree with the African bees' nest
So far away in space and time
Another world, another country, another language
The streets I walked to get to *mercado*
The house of my *suegra*
The speed bump we fell on…
My son, and me, and my soon-to-be born daughter

Streets and houses sprawl a wider web
Around the small Venezuelan city
Small, like Pittsburgh is small
My brother-in-law's farm, still the same
The baseball field where my son
First learned to play on a team
The soccer fields where my husband
Played and later coached
Remain unchanged over time

Ochoa, the veterinarian neighbor on our left
Abel, the boy on our right, both born February 29
We broke curfew to celebrate in the year of the riots
We knew it was wrong
But cared too much about friends and neighbors
To realize the danger we defied
The sting of tear gas still fresh in the air

Home, here and now
Blurred, unfocused pixels
Like my life these days

HOPE

Gripping tightness in chest
Throat constricts
Eyes disobey orders
    As tears sneak down cheeks
Equally afflicted
By beauty
Pain, agony, hope
    "Sensitive" some say

Like the first game
After the world stood still
Holding its breath
    For a while
Girls in a straight row
Visitors, officials, home team
Facing West
    Towards the flag

As the national anthem played
And the sun settled on the treetops
Geese from a nearby pond
    Took flight
Coming together in
Ascending formation
Completing their "V" above the
    Home team girls

Flying through uninterrupted sky
Honking in rhythm to the line
"Oh say does that Star - Spangled Banner
    yet wave?"
Answering the question as they
Flew above the fluttering flag
Over the trees, taking the sun
    With them

Bringing hope that life goes on.
Like a life lived intensely
Always running, loving, giving
Moving to keep things whole
    Abruptly cut short
gone too soon
Remembered daily
Missed always
    Made a difference

And yet life must go on

Like walking in the dark
With only the light of HOPE
And flickering names
    To guide the way
Remembering those who fought
And lost
And those who still fight on
    With hope for the future

Because life will go on

GLORY TO THE OUTRAGED PEOPLE

The cradle of my adulthood
Rocks precariously in the storm
Pulse hastens
With unforgotten panic
From decades ago

Gloria al bravo pueblo
Clamors valiantly for justice
World ignores
With uninterested blinders
For what they do not know

THE STILL NEST

Two pairs of mourning doves
Seeking safe haven
Sheltered front porch
Unchosen

One pair moved on
The other nested
A hanging basket
Precarious

Two parents
sat
Two weeks
hatched
Two eggs
fed
Two hatchlings
raised
Two nestlings

Two fledglings
Survived the nights of freeze
Days of ninety degrees
Swirl and twirl of gusty winds
left

The morning after
The storms cracked through
Flooding streets and yards
Two unrecognizable bodies
Are the babies gone or gone?

SEASONAL THREADS

Dozens of contrails stitch a patchwork sky
Warm autumn hues embrace unbound edges
Of visible horizons

Harvest tractor trails reap what was sewn
Crisp rusts and russets seep through the fabric
Of woodlands and streams

Roads, fences, and rails block out patches
Nature's palettes transform vast forests
Of speckled hills and heaving mountains

Shades of grey pillow above our heads
Shades of grey blanket below our feet
Lost in tangles of unwoven strands

Hours spent planning, piecing, and placing
Soft textures comfort offspring's successor
And aging progenitor

Keen senses contrive to spawn sentiment
Contrast and constancy blend together
Through various naps and grains

SLIP

foliage flips from
general greens to
vivacious vibrancy
before
flittering
groundward
unbalanced days
sharp
shrouded
crisp
dank
alive
undead
muting all that
speaks to me
diving downward
only to return
eventually to
delusions of adequacy

WE CAN NEVER GO BACK

go left
go right
go straight ahead
but don't stand still
and we can *never* go back

what might have been
what almost was
what was, but never should have been
what can't be redone
what can't be undone
and we can *never* go back

every step
      every act
            every word
                    determine who
            and where
      we are
today

COVERAGE

Misty blur of the new day's birth
Shrouded wonder
Of what is and what appears to be

Shades of the seen and the unseen
Woven together
In dream remnants and reality

Earth's query finds satisfaction
Canvassed above
As promises lead to destiny

LAYERS

Loss
Leads to
Leaps of faith
Leaving behind intrusive fears
Leftover from distant dark days
Lessons in strength bind forces together
Leading ongoing battles against shallowly buried uncertainties
Lingering doubt banished to absolute silence
Lean nearer to inner truths
Listen to struggling souls
Longing for renewed
Love of
Life

PART III

3RD EYE

stay or go
sniff or blow
wake or sleep
laugh or weep

do what you're told
and never doubt
stay in the lines
or venture out

rules
lines
law
order

follow the threads
floating behind closed eyes
decide what's true
and what are lies

empty darkness
or a flash of light
there is no way
to decide what's right

your rules…my choice
stay in line…wander out
break the law…use my voice
screw the order…scream and shout

in the end
we each must choose
whether we win
or whether we lose

THE PERFECT WORDS

Suddenly waking I hear
The perfect words
Pirouetting in my head

I should write them down
Now
Before I lose them
Now
Even if it is only 3:30 in the morning
Now…

Listening as they spin
Their perfection
So vivid
Repeating
Over and over
This time I know
I will remember
This time they won't
Escape

So strong…
They guard my dreaming mind
Keeping away the pain

Sleep is so hard
Can't stay there
The words keep coming
Flooding me into consciousness
Forcing me awake

This time the words must wait
They are clear and strong
They can wait
Eyes hurt

Ever elusive sleep is returning
So seldom does it come back
The words can wait
They have to

Suddenly waking I hear
The perfect words
As they wind their way

Away
Slipping into shadows
That reflect what they were
But not what they are
Where did they go?

I should have listened
I should have answered
I should have trapped them on paper

Flakes of eggshells
Crushed and crumbled
Nothing else is left

Tonight …if they call
I will answer

Sleep is overrated

REFLECTIONS OF A CHAOTIC LIFE UNCUT & SUBMITTED

The assignment seemed easy enough.
"Sit for
30 minutes
every day
and look at
'something'
Then, after a few
weeks
write a poem about…"

Easy? Sure.
Except…
for the part about 30 minutes
and the part about every day
and the part about a few weeks
hhmmm…all about time
all time that does not exist,
not in my world anyway.

But, I am not one to shirk an assignment.

I would have to really make an effort.

I would have to make time
(if I could do that
if I could make time…
and market it…
or save it in a bottle…)

I picked my sitting spot,
(an easy chair in the living room)

and I picked my "something"
(the lamp
on the table
between the chair and the couch)

and decided to get in my 30 minutes
every day
for weeks
(even if it had to be 5 minutes at a time)

I sketched that lamp
its shape
its position
and noticed something,
something that would be my *something*.

I could see everything else that was on the table,
reflected, distorted,
in the body of the lamp.

I also saw that it had been a while since I dusted.

I made copious notes on what I saw,
how some things changed,
and some never budged.

Time of tissues, tea and Tums,
brain games, books
drinks, magazines
papers, books
dust.

I knew what I could do,
what I *would* do.

I saw the chaos that is my life.

I had to explain to my family that
"yes I AM busy, and
no I'm not just staring into space.
It's my homework…"

And those 5 minutes at a time turned in real half hours.
(sometimes)
I even cleared the clutter
(a few times)
and dusted (a little) more often.

When the weeks were up
I wrote
"Tissues, tea and Tums"
with a bunch of
blah blah blah
in the middle and
"and the dust thickens daily."

It was not what I wanted
So I tossed it
And wrote…
And tossed…
And wrote…
And tossed
Repeatedly.

Then I realized
this was an assignment I did not want to complete.
complete = finish
finish = done
done = no more reason
to sit
and reflect
the reflection.

And so maybe,
I'll just skip this one,
make it last
so here I sit.

And the dust thickens daily.

Reflections of a Chaotic Life
Submitted

        And the dust thickens daily.

BURN

Burn long
Burn bright
Try to focus
Regain sight

Burn long
Burn bright
Such a struggle
Do what's right

Burn long
Burn bright
Fight the shadows
Of the night

Burn long
Burn bright
Through the darkness
To the light

Burn long
Burn bright
Fall in shadows
I just might

Burn long
Burn bright

THOUGHTS WHILE DRIVING

sunrise chases me, but rarely blinds me
in the rearview mirror
ahead, drooping blood-tinged clouds

fresh flesh flashes
on the wall at my elbow
hope it was a deer...not someone's dear

might not be a good idea to take notes
while driving
or pictures, like Friday

but as long as I don't look
I'll be fine
I may even capture the moment

I'm lucky like that

UNSETTLED

Restless

Gypsy blood is roiling

Letting go of things I don't

Want to unpack

Releasing

Rehoming

Renewing

Regoing

POWERLESS

In the darkest of times

Always a light

When power lines fail

Way

Truth

Light

Re-route –

In an instant

Life changes

Temporarily

Miss a show

Permanently

Lose all we know

DARK VISION

As a young child I practiced blindness
walking eyes closed
a game of what if
punishing toes and shins

As a teen I visited blindness
darkness took me
seconds at a time
knocking me down on stairs

As an adult I employed blindness
using skills learned
through stormy nights
of powerless dark rooms

Now I fear blindness
flashes of light
cracking my vision
through trails of sticky tears

PROTECTED PRISON

Faerie fluffs flutter me by
Whisk away my lullaby
With crowning ring round yonder moon
Sleep, I'll not be visiting soon

Leaves of three and lucks of four
Hold my steps from road to door
Labyrinth leaves rustling fall
Mushroom circles grand and small

From landed fence of unsquared rails
Danger for the fae prevails
Channel across hills, trees, roads
Rivers and mounds, shared abodes

When clouds caress ridges high
Passage resumes 'tween earth and sky
Festive feasts, fights for thrill
Dawn and dusk when air holds still

Faerie fluffs flutter me by
Whisk away my lullaby
With crowning ring round yonder moon
Sleep I'll not be visiting soon

THERE ISN'T AS MUCH

In the early days of my marriage
in Venezuela
I learned to do it by hand
with blue *"Las Llaves"* soap
and cold water
hanging it out to dry
hoping it would in the rainy season
much like the Amish in winter

Before our first child was born we got
a washing machine
like the one I grew up with
not like many others had
although I learned
to wash clothes that way too
when visiting those with wringer washers
like my grandma's aunt used to have

Life is easier now
Kids are grown
Less laundry
More time

I waste so much time

NOTES

1. Tomorrow's Yesterday (2017)
2. Controlled (2006)
   Tomorrow's Yesterdays
3. Generations Unseparated by Time and Distance (2006)
   Tomorrow's Yesterdays
   +Writing Success Conference Poetry Award 2012
   Poetry Nook Aug 2016
4. Getting Ready (2006)
   Tomorrow's Yesterdays
5. It Was Inevitable (2006)
   Tomorrow's Yesterdays
6. The One (2006)
   Tomorrow's Yesterdays
7. Mother's Language (2006)
   Tomorrow's Yesterdays
8. Identity Denied (2006)
   Tomorrow's Yesterdays
9. unshelved (2006)
   Tomorrow's Yesterdays
10. Quotes from My Mom for Future Reference (2015)
    * *Poetry Nook* Dec 2016
    +Writing Success Conference Poetry Award 2016
11. Baptisms and Burials (2016)
12. Cat Again – Never Again (2006)
    Tomorrow's Yesterdays
13. Of Death and Flies and Summer (2017)
    Silver Birch Press, Feb 2017
14. Getting the Picture (2017)
    +Best of Penn Writers District 4 Road Trip Conference 2017
    Silver Birch Press May 2017

15. Google Earth (2006)
    Scrawl 2007
    * *Poetry Nook* Aug 2016
    +Best of Penn Writers District 4 Road +Trip Conference 2016
16. Hope (2006)
    **Tomorrow's Yesterdays*
17. Glory to the Outraged People (2014)
18. The Still Nest (2017)
19. Seasonal Threads (2014)
    **Poetry Nook* February 2018
20. Slip (2016)
21. We Can Never Go Back (2005)
    **Mini-Scrawl* 2005
22. Coverage (2013)
23. Layers (2014)
24. 3rd Eye (2006)
    **Tomorrow's Yesterdays*
25. The Perfect Words (2003)
26. Reflections of a Chaotic Life – Uncut
    Reflections of a Chaotic Life – Turned In (2006)
    **Tomorrow's Yesterdays*
27. Burn (2003)
28. Thoughts While Driving (2011)
29. Unsettled (2018)
30. Powerless (2018)
31. Dark Vision (2017)
    **Postcard Poems & Prose* June 2017
    **Poetry Nook* Jan 2018
32. Protected Prison (2018)
    **Flutter Me By* (picture book to be published 2018/2019)
33. There Isn't As Much (2017)
    **Poetry Nook* Jan 2018

(year written)
*Denotes Publication
+Denotes Awards

ABOUT THE AUTHOR

Debra R. Sanchez (d.r. sanchez) has moved over thirty times... so far. She and her husband have three adult children, four grandchildren, as well as a cat and a dog. She leads and attends various writing groups in the Pittsburgh area and also hosts writing retreats and workshops.

Her bilingual picture book *And My Mother Cried/Y Mi Mamá Lloró* won The Author Zone TAZ Award for "Best Children's Book 2017" and her writing guide *Prompted, Prodded, Published* was awarded a TAZ Award in the business book category.

Her other writing has won awards at writers conferences in various genres, including children's stories, poetry, fantasy, fiction, and creative nonfiction. Several of her plays and monologues have been produced and published. Her work has been published in literary magazines, local newspapers, and anthologies.

For more information, visit her webpage:

www.DebraRSanchez.com
Follow her on Facebook: @DebraRSanchez
and Twitter: @DebraRSanchez

www.ingramcontent.com/pod-product-compliance
Lightning Source LLC
Chambersburg PA
CBHW031429040426
42444CB00006B/745